Fly With Poetry

An ABC of Poetry

Fly With Poetry

An ABC of Poetry

Written and Illustrated by Avis Harley

Wordsong/Boyds Mills Press

To the two Franks
with love and thanks

—A. H.

Text and illustrations copyright © 2000 by Avis Harley
All rights reserved

Published by Wordsong
Boyds Mills Press, Inc.
A Highlights Company
815 Church Street
Honesdale, Pennsylvania 18431
Printed in Hong Kong

Publisher Cataloging-in-Publication Data

Harley, Avis.
Fly with poetry : an abc of poetry / written and
illustrated by Avis Harley. 1st ed.
[48]p. : col. ill. ;   cm.
Summary: A collection of verse that provides examples of poetic forms.
ISBN 1-56397-798-2
1.Canadian poetry—Juvenile literature. 2. Children's poetry,
Canadian.
[1. Canadian poetry. 2. Poetry.] I. Title.
811.54 —dc21 2000 AC   CIP
99-63733

First edition, 2000
The text of this book is set in 15-point Clearface Regular.

10 9 8 7 6 5 4

Introduction

POETRY HAS BEEN AND ALWAYS WILL BE A PART OF US. Events in everyday life have been recited, chanted, and sung since the beginnings of language. In ballad or rap, sonnet or blues, poetry is the imaginative expression that illuminates something within each of us.

But many students, and adults, shy away from poetry, thinking it too complicated, remote, obscure—the baffling cousin to prose. This is understandable, for poems sometimes can be elusive and challenging and are as varied as the voices and cultures which create them.

Fly with Poetry introduces a rich variety of poetic forms and techniques—some handed down through the centuries, others comparatively new. Through poetry, with its myriad of forms, there is no limit to the imagination. Poets of all ages can explore and discover the delight and excitement of words and language structure, and enjoy creating new forms of their own.

This book is not a "how-to" on teaching poetic forms, but rather an introduction to the definitions of some of the wonderful tools available in the art of poetic expression. Exposing children to a variety of forms and techniques will expand their poetry horizons and give them new tools to release their thoughts and feelings.

An ideal way to use this book is to savor the playfulness of the poems, encourage the children to interact with the ideas, and discuss how the forms shape the reader's experience. Each poem is full of carefully-made choices which begin with the poet and continue with the reader. Students wishing to explore poetic forms should be encouraged to select those forms which excite their imaginations and enable them to express their thoughts more creatively.

It is best not to "back into" a poem by discussing a form before reading the poem. The delight is in the discovery. Readers and writers are invited to find the possibilities that the poem offers ... and then play with words ... experiment with forms. Extend. Invent. Have fun. Fly with Poetry!

—Avis Harley

Table of Contents

A becedarian

FORGOTTEN GIANTS:

Ancient
Bogs
Contain
Dinosaur
Eggs,
Forgotten
Giants
Hidden
Inside
Jurassic
Kingdoms.

Like
Memories
Never
Opened,
Prehistoric
Quagmires
Retain
Secrets.

This
Unknown,
Vanished
World,
X-tinct:

Yesterday's
Zoo.

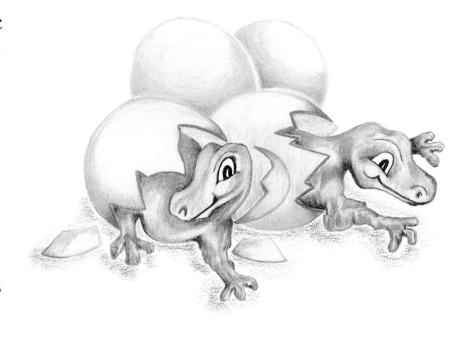

ABECEDARIAN: *an alphabetical poem that uses the letters A to Z in their proper order to form the first letters of every line.*

 **Acrostic**

EDITING THE CHRYSALIS

"At last," cried Butterfly,

Poised
Over its
Empty chrysalis,
"My final draft!"

Acrostic

A ROCK ACROSTIC

Inside	these	deep
tunnels	of rock	echo
soft	rhythms like	the
faint beat of	earth's	heart;
under this	ancient	layer
new stalactites	drip	steadily.

ACROSTIC (TRIPLE): *The first letters of the initial and middle words and the final letters of the last words have a meaning when read downward.*

Blank Verse

I'M A MYNA

I mimic noise, I imitate a voice,
I copy chat exactly as it is,
and when I shout: "ROLL OVER! SIT! LIE DOWN!"
a furry-one-with-fleas will leap about.
I love to tock to Clock and rap with Tap
who thrums his water fingers in the sink.
I'm like a magpie storing shiny things
for I collect the glitterings of sound.

BLANK VERSE: *a poem with ten-syllable lines, five accents in each, and no end rhyme.*

Cinquain

THE PEARL

Inside
An oyster shell
Glows a drop of moonlight,
Polished by the stars when it fell
Through night.

CINQUAIN: *usually a twenty-two syllable, five-line poem.*
1st line: two syllables, 2nd line: four syllables, 3rd line: six syllables, 4th line: eight syllables,
5th line: two syllables.

Doublet

HOW CAN YOU CHANGE 'SLEEP' INTO 'DREAM'?

Instead of falling into sleep
by counting sheep, I listen for rhythms
inside my head: the cheep of a chickadee,
rain on my cheek,
a murmuring creek,
the creak of new shoes,
or cats lapping cream. These are the rhythms
that flow through my dream.

DOUBLET: *a word is changed, one letter at a time, into another word and arranged vertically in the poem.*

End Rhyme

PERHAPS

"He's safe!" the Bronto players shout,
But Umpire Tritops yells, "You're out!"

"No way!" shrieks Number Forty-one
Who claims his tail-tip scored a run.

A fight breaks out between the teams;
The air is wild with dino screams.

Soon fans begin to lumber in,
Creating prehistoric din.

The skirmish spreads into the stand,
For days it rages through the land.

When all the dust had settled down,
Silence covered every town.

Perhaps this battle could be linked
To why the dinosaur's extinct.

Free Verse

TREE DANCERS

Winds
sweeping over pines
shape limbs into
rigid images:
tree dancers
locked
in frozen rhythm—
silent tango partners.

FREE VERSE: *lines of poetry that are written without a regular rhythm or rhyme scheme and are freed from any one metrical pattern.*

Ghazal

CARTOONS FOR RACCOONS

Raccoons slink on our porch at night
and watch us through the window light.

They crowd together, pressed up tight;
they seem to like this viewing sight.

Perhaps we're their T.V. What might
they see in us that would excite?

Raccoon Cartoons? Their choice is slight:
one channel without satellite.

But Human News, however trite,
appears to them to be just right.

Eight round eyes — intense, polite —
watch us watch them watch our delight.

Vis-à-vis we meet each night
to share this curious appetite.

GHAZAL: *a poem of couplets all using the same rhyme, and with the poet's name hidden in the final couplet.* *(vis-à-vis: face to face)*

Haiku

Cat preens in the sun,

Smoothing her ruffled fur robe;

The fleas are awake.

HAIKU: *a Japanese form of poetry consisting of three short lines with the middle line being slightly longer. The syllables are often arranged in a 5/7/5 pattern.*

Internal Rhyme

READING THE TREE

I need to read my family tree

upsidedown.

If I turn it around with the boughs in the ground,
then offshoots are roots
that show how I grow.

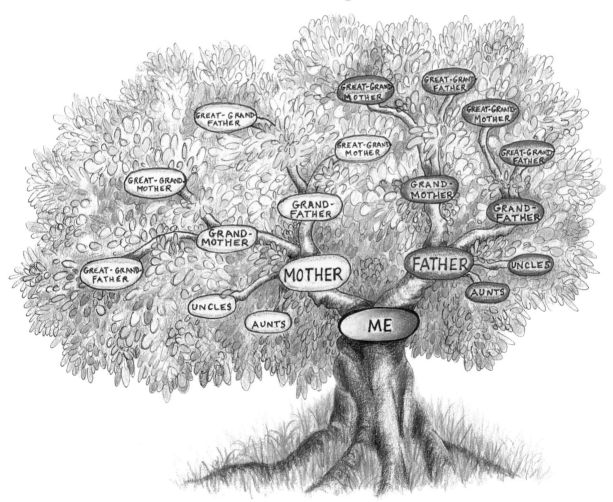

INTERNAL RHYME : *rhyme occurs within the lines.*

Jingle

THE THREE-LEGGED RACE

Willy-nilly millipede,

Leg-by-leg-by-leg agreed

To tie the race in record speed,

Willy-nilly millipede.

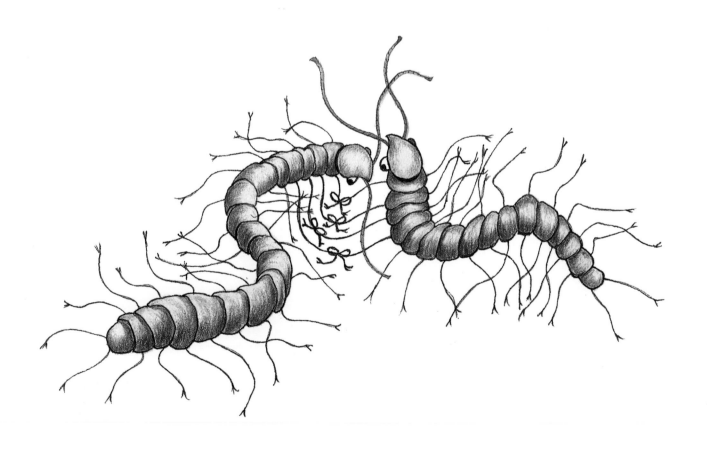

JINGLE: *verse designed to catch attention by the use of pronounced sound-repetitions and catchy rhythms.*

yrielle

BIRTHSTONES

How is it the salmon know
where to bury ruby roe?

Something signals when to go;
they journey homeward, rich with roe.

To birthstones of so long ago
the fish return to lay their roe.

Under currents, just below,
the jade green streams are jeweled with roe.

KYRIELLE: *a kyrielle is divided into couplets, each pair of lines ending with the same word which acts as the refrain.*

 Limerick

In the marsh lived a musical toad
who emerged from his muddy abode
and remarked, "Why, it's spring!
That's the time when I sing!"
and ballooned himself up to explode.

LIMERICK: *a five-line verse using the anapestic rhythm — lines 1, 2, and 5 rhyme and have three beats, lines 3 and 4 rhyme and have 2 beats.*

etaphor

CONNECTIONS

This shell is my phone
to call up the sea
and ask, "What's the news?
How's the family?"

I can hear songs of whales,
the surf in a roar,
and laughter of pebbles
teasing the shore.

When I miss the sea
in my small city home,
I connect up with Neptune
on shellular phone.

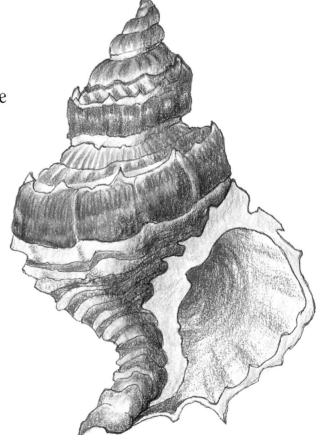

THE COLORING SPREE

Six felt pens went off to play
Into the world of Yesterday.

    They colored the rainbow and also the skies,
    They found stone statues and colored the eyes,
    They colored the flowers, especially the rose,
    They colored the nails on a Sphinx's toes,
    They colored in cracks on a castle wall,
    They found white parrots and colored them all,
    They added a touch to the autumn trees,
    And wrote: "Felt Rules!" on parchment leaves.

They had such fun on their coloring spree
There isn't much left in the pens for me!

Onomatopoeia

SMALL SOUNDS

Have you heard
small sounds of the world:

    a tippity-tap when a ladybird lands,
    the scrinching-scrunch of a slug crunching lunch,
    or the rumble of worm murmurs under the ground?

Have you heard
the small of the world?

ONOMATOPOEIA: *words which imitate sounds of objects or actions.*

Picture poem

FIRST JUMP

Climb on the high diving board, look
D
O
W
N
Knees knock
My jaws lock
Heart pumps
Fear thumps
Grip my toes
Hold my nose
P
L
U
N
— through the smooth blue sheet waiting below —
G
E
Splitting sunlight!
the bright
surface pierces
heart soars
sings tingles
eyes body
sting

PICTURE POEM: *the meaning is suggested by the arrangement of the words.*

Quatrain

LATER

My teacher said I should look up
this word: PROCRASTINATE.
I'll check it out when I get home,
it's just a little wait.

But after school my friends drop by,
we laugh and play and fight;
then suddenly it's dinner time,
I'll look it up tonight.

But now the television's on,
homework's looking bleak;
PROCRASTINATE can wait a bit,
I'll look it up next week.

QUATRAIN: *a four-line poem or stanza*

Rhopalic Verse

TAPESTRIES

Small spiders filigree
the garden greenery
with silken precision. Delicately, definitively,
they network tapestries
that capture
more
than morning's glorious
dew.

A BITE-SIZED SONNET

House

sleeps.

Mouse

creeps

in

through

thin

flue.

Spots

cheese;

stops.

Sees

cat.

SCAT!

SONNET: *a poem of fourteen lines with ten syllables in each line (except for the bite-sized version, which has only one syllable per line).*

The lines are often divided into the first eight (octave) and the last six (sestet).

Triolet

PHOSPHORESCENCE

Have you ever swum in a sea

alive with silver light

sprinkled from a galaxy?

Have you ever swum in a sea

littered with glitter graffiti

scribbled on liquid night?

Have you ever swum in a sea

alive with silver light?

36 **TRIOLET:** *an eight-line poem. Lines 1, 4, and 7 are identical; lines 2 and 8 are identical; lines 3 and 5 rhyme with the first line; line 6 rhymes with the second line.*

Uta

Tall delphiniums,

thirsty for a sip of blue

to fill their petals,

poke green stems into the sky

and drink their fill of sapphire.

UTA: *(also known as TANKA) — a five-line poem of Japanese origin. The syllables are sometimes arranged as 5/7/5/7/7, although variations occur.*

Villanelle

VILLANELLE: *a villanelle has six stanzas. The first five stanzas are three lines in length and the last stanza is four lines. The first and last lines of the opening stanza take turns*

COME, DRUM!

Come, drum! Sound out the day!
Your humdrum frame has much to tell.
Roll out your rhythms and sweep us away.

Pump out the heartbeat for jazz and ballet;
Kindle the dancers who spin under spell.
Come, drum! Sound out the day!

Pound out the surf; thunder the spray;
Answer the raging, roaring swell.
Roll out your rhythms and sweep us away.

Shake out the song in an old roundelay;
Echo those voices that rose and fell.
Come, drum! Sound out the day!

Crack open night with a fireworks display;
Explode into gold each shimmering shell.
Roll out your rhythms and sweep us away.

Dance in our veins and pulse in our play;
Exult in the language you know so well.
Come, drum! Sound out the day!
Roll out your rhythms and sweep us away.

repeating as the last line of the next four stanzas. They are then repeated as the last two
lines of the poem. The villanelle has a rhyme scheme of a-b-a.

39

Word Echo

DINOSAUR BONES

Older than words was the world of the Dino.
I know.

Why they all vanished is hidden from history.
A mystery.

Maybe nest-robbers gobbled the eggs clean away.
No way.

Some say that glaciers turned the earth icy.
I see.

But others believe in the meteor theory.
Eerie.

Do dinosaur bones make you feel a bit shivery?
Very!

Imagine the flesh that enveloped the skeleton!
A ton!

That's what's so thrilling about a museum!
You see 'em!

WORD ECHO: *a response poem where the last few syllables of a line are echoed in the following line.*

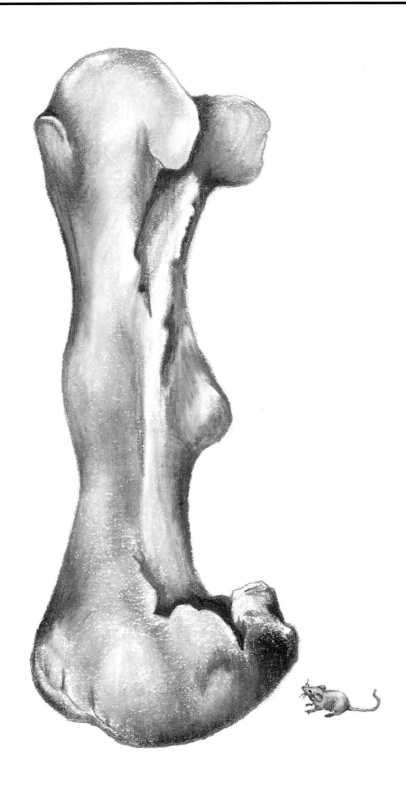

SEVEN HIDDEN ORANGES

Orange needs a rhyming friend,
nothing chimes with its end;
an orphan word left by itself,
all alone on the poetry shelf.

Peculiar ingenuity is needed for rhyming Orange:
"Three foreign
gentlemen, who all are in
jackets, stand on the shore
enjoying the waves that pour in
giant roaring
jets of foam from the sea."

Orange rhymes are shy; they hide inside a word
and are in jeopardy of never being heard.
Orange needs to find some friends
in other words with chimeless ends.

XCOGITO: *(from Latin "experimental thinking")*
*a poem containing experimental rhymes (e.g., "all **are in** jackets") for those words which*
cannot be rhymed by traditional means, such as "orange," "monarch," "circle," "silver," etc.

Your Poem

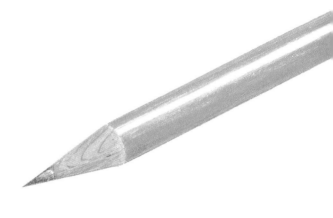

Zoophabet

ANTS TO ZORILLAS

Ants use antennae to seek out their tracks,
Beavers gnaw trees for their lodge,
Camels store food in the humps on their backs,
Dragonflies dazzle and dodge,
Elephant trunks furnish watery flings,
Flamingoes eat shrimp to keep pink,
Grasshoppers' ears appear under their wings,
Hummingbirds hover to drink,
Inchworms advance with a rear-ended loop,
Jellyfish sometimes can sting,
Kestrels catch lunch with a lightning-like swoop,
Larks love to warble and sing,
Moles tunnel intricate malls underground,
Newts thrive in ponds filled with weed,
Owls like to swivel their heads right around,
People can learn how to read,
Quetzals are gorgeous in feathery dress,
Rats have acquired a bad label,
Seahorse appears like a figure in chess,
Tortoise found fame in a fable,

ZOOPHABET POEM: *an alphabetical poem that deals with the naming of living things.*

Umber-birds thrive in the African wild,
Vipers can poison their prey,
Worms turn the soil when the climate is mild,
Xylophage chews wood all day,
Yaks grow in horns that are gracefully curled,
Zorillas are striped black and white;
        each zoophabet creature
                is
                        part
                        of
                                this
                                        world:
                                        unique,
                                        with
                                        its
                                        own
                                        copyright!

DAMS

Additional Poetic Forms

BALLAD

A ballad tells of a single, dramatic event. It is a story-song and is usually written in four-line verse, with the second and fourth lines rhyming. Any number of verses may be used.

CHANT

A chant is a poem intended to be read aloud with another person or a small group. Certain words, phrases, or lines create patterns of repetition that invite participation.

CLERIHEW

The clerihew is made up of two couplets of unequal length with outlandish rhymes. It often contains biographical notes about a famous personality. The person's name should appear in the first line.

COUPLET

The couplet is two linked lines of verse, usually with the same rhyme and rhythm, although not all couplets have regular line length.

DIAMANTE

The diamante is a poem consisting of seven lines.
Line 1: noun (one word)—subject is the opposite of the word in the last line.
Line 2: adjectives (two words)—describe subject in first line.
Line 3: participles (three words)— 'ing' or 'ed' words about subject in first line.
Line 4: nouns (four words)—
    two words are about subject in first line;
    two words are about subject in last line.
Line 5: participles: (three words)— 'ing' or 'ed' words about subject in last line.
Line 6: adjectives (two words)—describe the subject in last line.
Line 7: noun (one word)—subject opposite of the word in the first line.

EPIGRAM

An epigram is a brief, witty, and thought-provoking statement. In poetry, it is usually two or four lines in length.

LANTERNE

The lanterne is composed of five lines with the following syllabic count:

Line 1 — one syllable
Line 2 — two syllables
Line 3 — three syllables
Line 4 — four syllables
Line 5 — one syllable

LIST POEM (CATALOGUE POEM)

Items, events, activities, etc. are listed in rhymed or unrhymed lines. The lines have no fixed length and any number of items can be in the set.

NEWSPAPER POEM

Interesting words, phrases, or headlines are cut out of the newspaper and rearranged until a poem emerges.

PROSE POEM

A prose poem is without verse lines and appears in paragraph form. It is usually rich in imagery and often has a rhythmic quality.

QUINTET

A quintet consists of five lines. Poets may devise any rhyme scheme or have no rhyme scheme at all. The meter and line length are not fixed.

RIDDLE POEM

A riddle contains a puzzle or problem. When it appears in poetic form, it is usually rhymed.

SKELTONIC VERSE

Skeltonic verse is composed of short lines with rhymes that continue for as long as the poet wishes, changing only when the poet feels that particular set of end rhymes has been artistically exhausted.

TRIPLET (TERCET)

The triplet is a verse composed of three lines. It usually contains rhyme, and nearly always has the same rhythm throughout.

About the Author/Illustrator

Avis Harley grew up in British Columbia, Canada. She graduated with an MA and teaches poetry at the University of British Columbia in the Language Education Department. Ms. Harley has also been an elementary school teacher for many years.

She is married to Frank Harley and they have one son. Besides writing and drawing, Ms. Harley enjoys music, hiking, gardening, and cooking. She is an avid reader and belongs to two book groups.

This is her first book of poetry for children. The book grew out of a life-long interest in experimenting with words, rhythms, patterns and ideas.